Thank you!

Dan Webber
is

GENRE

FLUID

Published by Big White Shed, Nottingham, England
ISBN 9781916403550
Printed and bound in the EU by Booksfactory
Cover by Brett Maskill-Watts
Copyright © Dan Webber 2019
Made possible with funding from the
ERDF Big House Project

Genre Fluid

Having produced two spoken word shows to date, Genre Fluid is the culmination of three years of writing, touring and performing at various events and festivals across the country. Being constantly told you're a comic at poetry nights and a poet at comedy nights can be very confusing, as is the constant pressure to define yourself and your work. Genre Fluid is a study into labels in everyday life, in the arts and the LGBT+ community, written by Dan Webber (reluctant bear, attempted vegan).

> *Webber's set quickly enters an easy-going, natural flow, with sentimental musings on self, mental health, masculinity, appearance, and place, all delivered with a playful and occasionally giddy appeal.*
> **LeftLion Magazine, August 2018**

> *A roller coaster of laughs and heart breaks, with some of my favourite poems being, 'Anonymous at 6am' and 'Homo on the Rocks', very different in tone and style and yet both equally as captivating.*
> **Impact Magazine, August 2018**

GENRE FLUID – SET LIST

1) – introduction
Edinburgh – p7
Moobs – p9
Filth – p11
Friend of Dorothy – p14

2) – poems about boys
T – p18
Thief – p19
Prince – p20

3) – gay dating in 2019
Anonymous at 6am – p23
Escort – p24
Profile – p26
You Only Send Kisses When You're Horny – p28

4) – labels
First Impressions – p32
Child of the 90s – p34
Relax / Superheroes – p36
Paris is Learning – p38
Homo on the Rocks – p40
Some People Never Learn – p42
Still Learning – p44

5) – not being funny
17 Squared – p49
No Filter – p51
Sounds of the City – p52
Wonderland – p53
Happy Anniversary – p54

1) - introduction
Edinburgh
Moobs
Filth
Friend of Dorothy

Edinburgh

Edinburgh. Fringe. 2018.
It's 2am and it's my first night and I'm tired.
Stood pissing over a flyer that's been crammed down a urinal
And I don't care because I'm tired.
I'm so tired.
Everybody's tired.
Did I mention I'm tired?
Do you have a show?
Do you have a show?
What do you mean you don't have a show?
    I don't know?
Well, what do you do?
Are you a comic?
    Occasionally.
Are you a poet?
    Reluctantly.
Reluctantly? Hey mate, are you trying to be funny?
That's the problem.
I have no idea.
I'm not funny enough to be a comic,
and I'm not serious enough to be a poet,
I think I might be Genre Fluid.

When I started doing this I was on the bill of a charity night in Derby and before the show started the compere asked me if I wanted to be in the comedy section or the poetry section, and I had no idea.

I've spent so long convincing myself I am this mature, professional and grown up spoken word artist, so with that in mind this is a mature, professional and grown up poem. About man boobs.

Moobs

On a warm summer's day
Why is it OK to have Moobs on display but not boobs?
Who made it this way?
Who are these anti-tit hypocrites
Who sit on committee and banned the titty?
More's the pity,
You go to any city, here or abroad
On a warm August day
And you'll see slap-heads and beer-bellies strutting away.
Man boobs on display
Without a care in the world
But say you're driving round town or walking around
And you see a mother breastfeeding her child?
Some people go wild!
Becoming enraged like it's strange
They completely lose their minds
Mankind has worse crimes than showing some nipple at lunchtime.
Are we as a nation so against titillation?
Society teaches that nudist beaches are OK
But breast-feeding in public is wrong in every single way
But
If breast is indeed best, I say let's put to the test
a new page 3
Introducing Phil from Coventry
He's a heavy-set man 48EE
His interests include beer and misogyny
I know what I'd rather see...

I think it's important to start the show with a content warning: my poetry's a bit shit.

Genre Fluid is a study into labels in the arts, in everyday life and in the LGBT+ community, so with that in mind here is a list of unacceptable labels we will not be using for the next 55 minutes -

slides 2-15: unnacceptable labels

GAY, when used in a negative context
QUEER, when used in a negative context, or to get Arts Council Funding
FEM
SISSY
STRAIGHT THIN
STRAIGHT THIN BUT GAY FAT
DADDY
SUGAR DADDY
SUGAR BABY

And the most unacceptable label of them all - EMERGING ARTIST.

I'm very grateful for you all coming tonight to be honest I'm very grateful to be here at all because after my last gig I got in trouble with the law, I used a label the law didn't like - this is called Filth

Filth

I'm sorry
I'm sorry
I'm so, so, sorry
I'm sorry for the obvious offence my words have caused
I understand now, referring to an officer of the law as
Filth down an open microphone
At a family fun day was unacceptable
Even in jest
And you have every right to be upset
Please don't arrest me
I'm not cruising for a bruising or looking for a night
in the cells
I like my anal sex to be consensual
Look at me, no, no really, look at me
We both know I won't last long on the inside
I'm vegan
I love prison films but I'm more yellow belly than Green
Mile
I would have surely got shanked in the Shawshank
Redemption
Apologies, I'm attempting to use humour to mask a
tense situation
Here's one for you,
How many policemen does it take to screw in a
lightbulb?
Just one, because they are more than capable, and
valued members of society
Ok I'll come quietly
But before we go
Can I just nip home and delete my browser history?
And my tumblr page?
There's stuff on there my mother doesn't need to see...

My browser history is made up of mostly tops, bottoms and twinks, now for anyone who may be unfamiliar with the vernacular we've created this handy beginner's guide

Tops are people who prefer to penetrate during anal sex, as in 'to give'

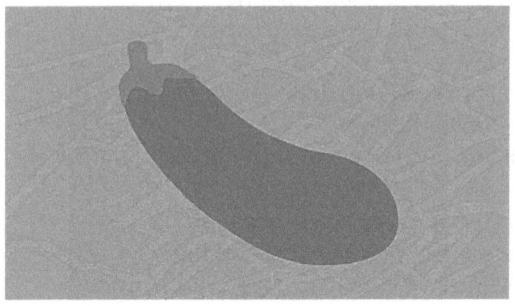

slide 17: aubergine/eggplant pic

Bottoms, bottoms are people who prefer to be penetrated during anal sex, as in 'to receive'

slide 18: peach pic

And Twinks, well the definition of Twinks is the following...

TWINKS

"Attractive, boyish-looking, young gay men. The stereotypical twink is 18-22, slender with little or no body hair."

slide 19: Twink definition

Twinks are the people I'm constantly trying to have anal sex with. This is my Twink.

slide 20: Twink pic

Like all my Twinks I found him on the internet. Word to the wise, never Google
- gay twink cartoon -
you'll never see Tom Daley in the same way again.

Friend of Dorothy

I must remember that my sense of humour doesn't
always travel well
And when I see a fellow homosexual they may not be as
open or accustomed to the jokes I'm partial to
We're discussing musicals (that's clue one)
On a Christmas gig in full costume, he introduces
himself as 'Twinkie the Elf'

(that's clue two)

slide 21: Twink Elf

And I perk up like a horny meerkat
I'm attempting to flirt
My style is still very much play-ground
If I like you I will pull at your hair
and tug at your skirt
Because I'm not mature enough even now to
simply ask you out for a drink after work
In spite of this, it's going alright
He explains his favourite musical is The Wizard of Oz
And I say "of course it is because you're clearly a friend
of Dorothy"
He recoils
His whole body pulled backwards as if sucked into the
cyclone in Kansas

slide 22: Grumpy Twink Elf

"What's that supposed to mean?" he quite rightly asks

I stutter, the only sounds coming from my jingle jangle boots
Which I wish were ruby slippers so they could whisk me away
"It's OK" I explain "I like guys, so I can say that to you, I wear rainbow laces in my work boots"

You ever hear something you've said out loud and realise how profoundly dumb it sounds?
This is my background music

I apologise again and again, and think of all the other men I've lambasted in poetry for just this kind of behaviour

He follows me on twitter, offering a glimmer of hope.

slide 23: @Dan_Webber_Poet

2)- poems about boys
T
Thief
Prince

I've been doing this for the past four years and I've been very lucky, I've performed at festivals and events all over the country.

I was doing a gig in Birmingham last summer and I was on the bill with this incredible spoken word artist, and before the show we're both sat in the green room and we start chatting and she asks me, "what do you write about?" And I think "Ok this is my one chance to make a really good impression" so I say "Me? I write about all the important stuff, I write about love, I write about life and I write about relationships" and my mate who was stood next to me at the time said, "no you don't, you don't write about love, life and relationships, you just write about boys"

These are some poems about boys

slide 25: Twink pic

T

You stand there with your quaffed hair smiling at me
And straight away I can see that you, you are trouble
Double trouble. No, no, make that triple
And after a tipple I'm looking at you
through a slight haze
And I'm amazed that we're here just having a beer
And yes, I am a bit pissed, but
I've missed this company
It's only now I realise how much I enjoy
spending time with this boy
And I'm starting to hope
Now hope is a very dangerous thing
Hope is a rhythm that makes your heart sing
But it's followed by a sting
 - a fear I'm falling.
I never expect
But do I detect a slight flirtation?
A glance? A touch?
Am I trying too hard or looking too much?
Seeing things that are just not there
Well, tonight for a change I simply don't care
Give me this second,
Mine now to keep
Buy me that pint and take the last leap because yes
Yes, yes, yes, yes, yes
You are trouble
And I fucking love trouble.

Thief

You're wearing false glasses
And the fake plastic lens reflects the festival lights
Masking your eyes
So, I focus on your smile
And we're told just to look
Instructed not to touch but to notice every detail of the person stood before us
The patterned bag
The beaten docs
The slightly hipster woven top
The half drank can of gin and tonic held discreetly by your side
Underneath the no drinking sign
"This isn't mine" you whisper
"nothing is, I'm just a thief"
And what I wouldn't give for another stolen moment like this.

slide 26: Twink in comedy specs

Prince

To the third boy I ever brought back to my parent's house
I have to be at work at 8
And this is a mistake
But I tell you, you are the most beautiful boy I've ever seen
And I mean it
A Prince among men
Tonight, I have lucked out
Punching high above my weight
And I've got more chance of messing this up than of making love
But nothing's going to stop me trying even just the once
You tell me you're not used to being kissed
So I make it my mission to change this
Afterwards, I ask you to stay
But you pick up your keys and your phone
and you leave anyway
And I don't know if this is a one-shot hook up
But as I sit and sip my whiskey and pep
I hope I get to see you again
Text me when you get in yeah?
But he never did.

slide 27: Twink in crown

3) – gay dating in 2019
Anonymous at 6am
Escort
Profile
You Only Send Kisses When You're Horny

By now some of you may have realised I'm a guy that likes guys, and if you hadn't worked that out you've not been paying enough attention.

I've been single, on and off, for the last four years, and I've started using dating apps.

Give me a cheer all the single people…

Give me a cheer if you're single and using dating apps?

So many liars in the room, but for those who are brave enough to admit it I need your help, how do you do it, how do you get to know someone through a screen, because I just can't manage it?

I was talking to a guy on Tinder a few weeks ago and I asked him if he was left wing or right wing and he told me he was vers top. Not a joke.

This is an ode to dating apps and it's called Anonymous at 6am

Anonymous at 6am

Hey guy,
Just to clarify
Never have I ever given the impression
Or mentioned that I would be A-OK
With a 6am message to say I am invited round for fun
And I should totally come
I yawn, as you offer arse crack at the crack of dawn
And I am forlorn at your approach
Encroaching closer and closer to the creepy
I'm still sleepy I don't need this
And yet still you persist
No, I don't know who you are
I didn't fix your sister's car
Nor do I work at Butterfly Reservoir
You have me mistaken
I haven't taken you out for a drink before
I'm not that guy you think you saw
Honestly? I'm not sure what I'm looking for, but I'm guessing it's not you
And you're continuously pressing the send key
Bombarding me
And I'm still politely saying no
This persistence isn't flattering
Nor is the smattering of faceless nudes
Included in your flirtatious text
I gather that you're horny yes but I'm not feeling this
No worries, he sends
And blocks me, like I've done something wrong…


```
This is gay dating in 2019.
```

Escort

slide 29: escort text

I don't mean to sound funny but are you prepared to pay?
Cause I don't come cheap
I've been kind up to now but if you're going to keep texting there's a fee
And if you're expecting full sex the price starts at £150
Anything less we can negotiate
By the way
I don't kiss
Or do piss
Or any of that freaky shit
I've got limits
But you can make me your bitch
You can punch me,
kick me,
choke me out
Then transfer funds directly to my PayPal account
So, Daddy, what do you want?

This is gay dating in 2019

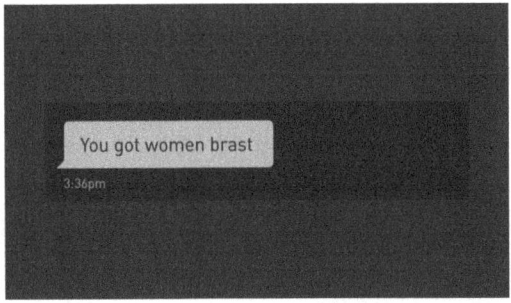

slide 30: Grindr

This is gay dating in 2019

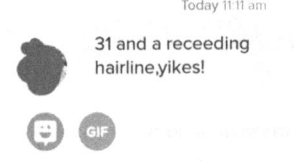

slide 31: Tinder

This is gay dating in 2019

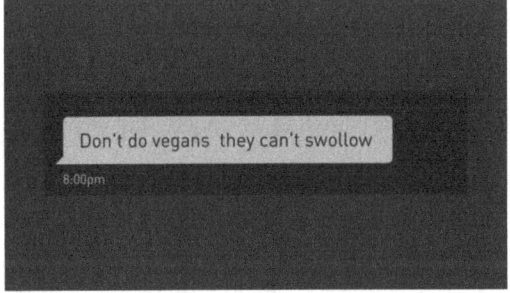

slide 32: Grindr 2

Profile

Straight guy seeks sugar daddy
Needs to be discreet
Complete satisfaction guaranteed
Will do anything you want for the right price (wink wink)
Photos sent only to the right guy (wink wink)
Will not respond to taps
Fats, fems and Asians need not apply (crying face emoji)
Follow me on Instagram
Donate to my Onlyfans
Snapchat and WhatsApp listed below

This is gay dating in 2019
Staring at the same screens, night after night
Wading through the knee-high bull shite
Swiping right through pictures
filtered within an inch of their life

More bots than bottoms
Dorian gays rotten to the core
Sans thesaurus
More well-versed in dick than dictionary
Shaved bare because hairy is so… urgh

Did I mention I'm a Christian?
Then act like it
Spewing out hate like a preacher
Oh wait, you're a Christian of course that explains it
Self-loathing
Self-loathing everywhere

Don't talk to me
Don't talk to me if you judge only on looks
Don't talk to me if you'll message me across a room

rather than speak face to face
In case of what people might say if they see us together
Don't talk to me if you can't get past this
Because this might be me on a good day.

And don't talk to me if you only send
kisses when you're horny.

You Only Send Kisses When You're Horny

You only send kisses when you're horny
And being at your beck and call was starting to get boring
You had the chance for this to advance, but you told me you wanted to keep things
"casual"
Well I'm done with that, I'm dressing smartly for a change
Trying not to arrange a date that I know isn't going anywhere
Just because I'm so damn scared of being alone
Or of staring at my phone all night
Wondering who else is awake at this time, and feeling like this.
You only send kisses when you're horny
And I should know by now that cross is there to warn me
But I'm still making mistake after mistake
Taking whatever is offered without question,
Without hesitation, without consequence or recompense
In an attempt to feel a little less like me
Wrapped in an embrace I can pretend is real
Albeit briefly
And I always say that this time, is the last time
Until the next time, and the next time, and the next time
When I hear that message chime and I'm there
Right back by your side, looking you dead in the eye and thinking
"what are we doing? Ruining a friendship, we both know this is never going to be a relationship and although you call me babe, I wasn't born yesterday so please, don't treat me this way"

You only send kisses when you're horny.

4) – labels
First Impressions
Child of the 90s
Relax / Superheroes
Paris is Learning
Homo on the Rocks
Some People Never Learn
Still Learning

I always worry because I only seem to write after I get laid, which is why it's taken me four years to come up with 55 minutes of material.

It feels like dating apps are the only way to meet people these days, but I hate using them.

I hate dating apps because I hate being stereotyped, on paper I am a bear.

slide 34: bear pic

Oh sorry, wrong slide.

BEAR

"A term used by the gay community to describe a husky, large man with facial and body hair."

slide 35: bear definition

I call myself a reluctant bear

I hate that label, the idea that I can be summed up in a four letter word, which is ironic because as much as I hate stereotypes I only date Twinks or at least try to.

During research for this show I actually found out Twink is acronym for Teenage, White, Into No Kink, so I don't even like Twinks, I like Tiks - Twenty-somethings into kink

With dating apps you don't get the full picture.

I can turn on an app on my phone and know within seconds who else in this room is using the app, what they are looking for, if they are top or bottom, sub or dom, in a committed or open relationship, in some cases any kinks or fetishes they enjoy and how far away they are from my exact location.

I can do that right now, anybody nervous?

But even with all that information I still won't know the person.

Its difficult to get to know someone in a culture so obsessed with the visual.

>   *NO FATS*
>   *NO FEMS*
>   *NO ASIANS*

slides 36-38: 'NO' words

First Impressions

Don't take this the wrong way but we specialise in
making guys look more appealing
And with a few simple procedures we can easily clear
up your problem areas
Could I interest you in a deep tooth cleaning?
Citrus skin peeling?
Or of course, for the more adventurous, there's always
anal bleaching
We teach a five-point hygiene plan to make you the man
we know you can be
Because everyone knows beauty is only skin deep
And you'll never meet anyone worthwhile
unless you look just the same as the picture on your
profile
I don't normally approach people like this on the street,
But for you I'm willing to make the exception
Did I mention today we have 25% off?
Here, take my card, do drop me a line and we'll get you
sorted out in no time
Don't thank me it's fine, I'm happy to help.

Last year I was on a night out in Derby, and the morning after the night before I awoke to a message on my phone from a guy I'd briefly spoken to on a dating app which read "saw you in town last night, you look like an even bigger pussy in person".

There's been so much talk about limiting social media to children and young adults to try and improve mental health, why are we not doing the same thing with Grindr and Tinder?

This is gay dating in 2019

Child of the 90s

When I was younger
The way to find gay men was through MSN
Or via online chat
Perusing a room, naively assuming everyone was who they claimed to be
Searching gay porn on AOL at quarter to three in the morning out of teenage curiosity and wanking furiously
In sex education, homosexuality wasn't mentioned, wasn't discussed
You were just thrust into this confusing world of not liking girls and not really understanding why
Preferring the company of guys and realising that one mate was really, really, really fit
But not knowing how to react to it
See I was born on the cusp
In a backwards town,
Just before this rush of emerging equality
I remember people younger than me coming out and being astounded by their bravery
Because I didn't realise there was support there for people like me
This glorious LGBTQ+ community
I'm in my 30s and even now there's a part of me that still struggles with my sexuality
At parties, I felt the need to pretend in front of old friends
As conversations always end the same
You're seeing someone great! What's her name?
Her name
They assume
And suddenly I'm alone in a crowded room
And I know if I came clean it wouldn't change a thing
But what if it did?
There's still that thought in my mind, this sand in my eye

Would people treat me differently if they knew I liked guys?
But in time, that's getting better, I'm getting better.
On New Year's Eve 2016
I told my oldest friend I preferred men to women
And he was livid
Not because I liked guys
Because I had lied to him for all these years
I'd never told him when I was most happy.


```
That got a bit deep, wasn't it?
Let's just a take a second, everyone
breathe in... breathe out
Breathe in... and breathe out
Breathe in... and breathe out

And relax.
```

slide 40: Frankie says

Relax/Superheroes

The Frankie Goes to Hollywood Relax Music Video
Now for me this has been here since dot one but for you it's brand new
And I can see you shifting awkwardly
Sat in front of YouTube,
Trying to work out if you approve or not
Now, I know you very well
And I know you, you're no prude
And I know there's stuff in that video that you'd no doubt like to do
But that's not why I showed you
To me this is just another one of my dated cultural references,
A costume worn at an 80s fancy dress
But I forget you're only 19
And your history is somewhat limited by RuPaul's white washed hall of fame walls
Yes, Shangela was robbed
Yes, Manilla was robbed
Where do I begin
I remember watching Devine sing
on Top of the Pops 2

After the Simpsons and being mesmorised
Inundated with questions and emotions and then came
Rocky Horror
Tim Curry deflowering my curiosity
on late night Channel 4
B Movie grainy film ended,
and I begged for an encore
I told my dad that I didn't realise people could dress like that
I was 14
And I'd just seen the film which would define my late teens
That spark of life, rife within me
Goth boots and nail varnish
I used to quote that film word for word, line for line
And I'd try to do it now but I haven't got the time (warp)
Richard O Brien went from Crystal Maze host to saviour,
I'm not transsexual or even from Transylvania
But that late-night double feature taught me
That sexually and in life you really can be whatever the hell you want to be
So stop dreaming, and try me.

It's like my brother, my brother is a secret ladyboys lover.

slide 41: Lady Boy's pic

What did you think I meant?

Paris is Learning

My brother is a secret ladyboy lover
He claps his hands with glee as they move majestically and fantastically across the stage
Taking videos to send his mates
And he's not the only one
All around us people are watching the show through their phones which I don't condone but you know
And amongst the sequins and the killer heels I'm getting all the feels
because my family are altogether, which never seems to happen these days
And my brother, once this narrow-minded straight guy, has taken the plunge and is now having the time of his life
And I've had two bottles of wine so I am on cloud 9
Yes qween werk!!

Later on in the pub,
He turns to his big bruv and asks
Dan, are you sure they all had cocks?
Forcing me to drunkenly explain about the tuck.

When I'm not doing this I do a lot of shows for kids, different material obviously, but I was doing a show in Leicester last Easter and on the first day of rehearsals our leading man spent a good 95% of that first day making some really inappropriate homophobic comments and remarks, and I thought, 'I'm not having this,'so that night I rang the producer and she said "it's fine, thank you for letting me know, I'll talk to him, leave it with me, I'll talk to him".

So, the next morning comes and I walk back into the rehearsal room and to his credit he comes straight over, arms open wide and says, "Dan, Dan, I am so sorry, I had no idea, I didn't mean to offend you,you don't act like the rest of them"

Now, I had a choice.

I could have punched him in the face, but I didn't, after work I took him for a pint and calmly and quietly explained what an absolute cunt he was being.

This is called "Homo on the Rocks"

Homo on the Rocks

I'm at a house party playing catch up
Starting to feel the effects of a few cocktails and I set sail back to the bar
I'm stood, looking over the booze trying to choose when this guy next to me says
"Oi mate… mate…. Mate… You don't want that drink, that drink is a gay drink"
Now, I've had a few sherries and I'm feeling pretty merry
Perhaps a touch more unsteady than I care to admit
But I reckon I could still hit this motherfucker if it comes to it
"A gay drink?" I reply, manic twitch in my eye
And I see the guy's face drop
And before anyone can stop me, I say
"do you know exactly who you're talking to?
I'm Grindr's finest, the only cocksucker in the room
And for you to assume that my choice of drink in any way reflects my sexuality
Is a travesty
It's 2019
Where have you been and what have you done and what can I do to help you
Overcome this belief that gay means bad or inferior in any way
It's sad really."
He apologises for any offence and I spent the next twenty minutes furiously texting my friends
In the morning, he may not remember,
liquor loosens lips
But I hope before the next time he opens his mouth, he thinks.

Full disclosure, I wrote that poem about
three years ago, and I just update the
year every year, so in 2020 I'm screwed
cause it breaks the rhyme, but this next
poem I wrote about three months ago and
I'm sorry to say, not everybody thinks.

Some People Never Learn

He turns his nose up at the vegan homosexuals 'banging on' on stage
And claims that bacon for breakfast should be every man's birth-right
And I let it slide, not wanting to cause a fuss
With a dry uncomfortable smile, I leave the room and put distance between us for the rest of the gig
Cause this is work me,
Professional me,
Head down, don't rock the boat me
And it's only two days, so really,
how bad can it really be?
When it's time to leave, it's just us guys and he thinks he's in like-minded company
Complaining about his digs for the night
"Haven't you heard, they let Trannies in now"
That word
That word, so casual in his vocabulary,
like pausing for breath
My colleagues stir either side and feel me tense instantly their eyes shift apologetically away
They expect me to say something, but I don't
(don't make a fuss)
I am dumbfounded
(head down, don't rock the boat)
I stand and shake the hand of a man I have no respect for and thank him for his help
While on the inside I'm angry at myself
for not speaking up
For not calling him out

My father tells me it's to be expected
That certain men of a certain age think a certain way
and there's nothing we can do to educate them

So I shouldn't let it get to me
But it does
Because if no one speaks, nothing ever changes.

There are times I stand on stage and worry about offending my audience, worry about the points I'm raising and how comments could be mistaken or misconstrued –

"You never talk about consent in your poetry?"

"Have you never considered the term Genre Fluid could be offensive to someone nonbinary?"

Valid points all – but small in comparison to the day to day, throw away homophobia and transphobia we are currently faced with.

Still Learning

I don't identify as anything other than 'guy'
But I try to use correct pronouns where I can
I've stopped saying "hey man" or "girl please"
Because this world is rift with fluidity
And these members of our community deserve to be seen with the same visibility
As you see me standing here
I have a long, complicated history with the word queer
Queer to me, is shouted down school hallways and whispered by groups of teens
Queer is obscene, queer is banter and gossip and ignorance
But I understand, like many words before it, queer has been reclaimed
I stand on stage and talk about my sexuality because it's the only way I can
There're times I still can't
Sixth Form
First boyfriend, first dalliance
Too scared to come out
too scared to hold his hand in my father's car
Texting words across rooms I didn't dare say out loud as much as I wanted to
I remember the first time I smelt of you
Too scared to go too far
Too scared to commit
Too scared to accept and admit that I was a guy that liked guys
Cause I'd seen how people treated guys that liked guys
How people spoke to and spoke about guys that liked guys
You don't get it
You still don't get it
We don't get our awkward teenage years

growing in time with our peers
We have to find ourselves all over again
It's like puberty take two
So forgive me, cause I'm still finding the boundaries.

5) – not being funny
17 Squared
No Filter
Sounds of the City
Wonderland
Happy Anniversary

Like me, I'm not always sure where this show fits.

Last year I was applying for festivals and I applied to perform the show at a local Comedy Festival, and the organiser emailed back and said "Hi Dan, thank you for your application, we love the idea of the show but we don't really do poetry, have you considered..?"
And they gave me the name of a poetry festival, which I applied for, and the organiser emailed back and said "Hi Dan, thank you for your application, we love the idea of the show but we don't really do comedy, have you considered..." they then proceeded to recommend to me the comedy festival I had applied for in the first place.

It's a vicious circle.

During development last year I did this show at two different venues, the first venue described me as a mid career artist, and the second venue as an emerging artist (this was in the space of a week) that second venue three years ago also described me as an emerging artist when I performed there with my first show unintentionally suggesting in three years I had done nothing to 'emerge'.

Emerging. Mid-career. Labels

(slides 43 – 61: Labels)

But what do they mean?

Emerging — ok to still be living in your parents house

Mid career — not ok to still be living in your parents house

Emerging - probably doesn't know what they are doing

Mid-career — really should know what they are doing by now but probably doesn't

Emerging — Skint

Mid-career — What's less than skint

Emerging — You're 17

Mid-career — You're not 17 anymore

17 Squared

You're not 17 anymore.
You can't dress the same teenage Boheme
And expect the same respect
As other members of the management team
I still feel like I should be making the tea
But instead people are looking at me expecting answers
And I'm like, have you seen me?
Fuck-Up extraordinaire,
Still get my kicks watching Netflix
and re-runs of Fresh Prince of Bel-Air
Is this my life?
Is this my career?
The TV made it clear by now
that I should have a wife and kids
And know all the important grown up things like taxes
And how to wire a plug
But I still struggle with changing a bulb
The light above my head is yet to flicker
As everything falls into place
I just want to keep doing events
Events without the council politics
Events without the 'my dick is bigger than your dick' mentality
Without the stumbling blocks
I just want to get to the point where I can walk into a restaurant
And not worry about the cost.
Events management is the 5th most stressful job.

I am in events management and at the start of last year I was programming for a new festival about positive mental health and the importance of wellbeing, and at the same time I was struggling with perhaps the worst mental health I've had in a long time, so the timing was fantastic, and to top it off I was also appearing as the Mad Hatter in an Alice in Wonderland show, so I think I brought it on myself.

One of the ways I know when I'm not feeling great is I lose my filter, I start making inappropriate comments and jokes I'd never normally make. Like calling a policeman filth at a family fun day. I get so nervous and worked up about what I might say that I just stop speaking, which for a spoken word artist is far from ideal.

No Filter

The man on the phone asks if I'm depressed
Suggesting my chipper tone is masking some deep inner distress
And he's only cracking wise but he's totally right
And in that moment, I despise him
And his quite frankly lucky fucking guess
I don't speak
Even when I do speak, I don't speak
More concerned with how much you're repeating yourself
Or how much you're drinking on a Friday night
Than to shine that light back upon myself
To discuss my own mental health
It's my marbles Alice
I think it might be time to get some help.

Sounds of the City

When chaos rains down
and you drown in the sounds of the city
Take a second
Learn to reflect and remember
To ground yourself
Breathe deeply
Repeat as necessary
Yes, things are scary
And unexpected
Undetected curveballs fall constantly
But honestly, if life were a straight line and you were always on time
You wouldn't find half the answers to the questions
Or the people you have learned so much from
You are not the only one who struggles,
We are all weighed down by our own troubles
Chained to our own boulders
Yet silently we solider on
Not wanting to be a burden
But I am certain people care about you
And should you choose to,
And believe me you should choose to,
Tell them, tell them and they will care
And listen
And support
For we are the human race and this is what we do best
There is no test to fail, no right or wrong
Pour your favourite drink and put on your favourite song
Take that second
Never second guess
You are blessed simply by just being here
The alternative is a lot less attractive
Remember that.
Some good people didn't make it this far

Who you are and where you are is where you are
supposed to be
I believe this wholeheartedly
Things will get better
Just you wait and see.

When I'm at my lowest, I always seem to find
something to remind me what a wonderful
world we live in and this particular time
I found it in Asda in Sutton in Ashfield.

Wonderland

Teenage boy applying lip gloss in a supermarket mirror
"So, then he called me queer and I was like, yeah and?"
His friends giggle like it's no big deal
Stealing from the samples, they trade eye liners
And ever so slightly, the world changes.

Happy Anniversary everybody

Happy Anniversary

Daniel,
Daniel,
Daniel,
Yes, I am calling you Daniel because I am trying to be serious
I am writing to you, from the future
It's a bit like Doctor Who,
Or Terminator 2 with less budget,
Less special effects and less box office revenue
You popped up on my time hop today
Stood on a bridge near Tyneside
With a much thinner waist and a much fuller hairline
Wearing that Spiderman hoodie,
you never wear any more
And you were happy, smiling
There's no point denying you wasn't,
because you were
I should know, I was there
The man behind the lens, your then boyfriend
you think is the love of your life.
He's not, but he might have come close
Oh, heads up, when that ends it's really going to hurt
but it's totally worth it
You write poetry now
This is a poem
I know right!
I was as surprised as you are
But pay attention because I don't have long
There's going to be days when you want to give up.
Give up and vanish into thin air
When the pressure of living becomes too much,
and you think no-one cares
And the harsh truth is, not many people do

Everyone's got their own shit they're going through
But there's a special few, so keep an eye out
Work on your stubbornness
Work on your attitude
Never be cruel or cowardly
Peter Capaldi
Sorry spoilers! Spoilers!
And when it comes to poetry
Never write one of those self-indulgent 'letters to my younger self' poems
But if you must, never perform it
No one should be forced to sit through one of those

slide 63: Young Dan pic

Oh, and one final thing, one day a compere in Derby is going to ask you if you want to be in the comedy section or the poetry section and you will have no idea, and that's absolutely fine with me.

Please note:
images used in Powerpoint slides are author's own or are license free, except for slide 17 and 18 (eggplant and peach) which are licensed under the Creative Commons Attribution 4.0 International license.

Attribution: Mozilla